Dragonflies

by Cari Meister

ABDO
Publishing Company

visit us at
www.abdopub.com

Published by ABDO Publishing Company, 4940 Viking Drive, Suite 622, Edina, Minnesota 55435. Copyright © 2001 Abdo Consulting Group, Inc., Pentagon Tower, P.O. Box 36036, Minneapolis, Minnesota 55435 USA. International copyrights reserved in all countries. No part of this book may be reproduced in any form without written permission from the publisher.

Printed in the United States

Illustrators: Edwin Beylerian, Carey Molter

Cover photo: PhotoDisc

Interior photos: Animals Animals, Corbis Images, Peter Arnold, Inc., PhotoDisc

Editors: Tamara L. Britton, Kate A. Furlong

Design and production: MacLean & Tuminelly

Library of Congress Cataloging-in-Publication Data

Meister, Cari.
    Dragonflies / Cari Meister.
       p. cm. -- (Insects)
    ISBN 1-57765-461-7
    1. Dragonflies--Juvenile literature. [1. Dragonflies.] I. Title.

QL520 .M357 2000
595.7'33--dc21

00-056883

Contents

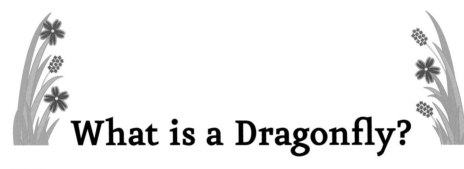

What is a Dragonfly?

There are more than 5,000 kinds of dragonflies. They are in the scientific family Odonata. Dragonflies have lived on Earth for millions of years. They used to be bigger than they are today. Fossils show that some dragonflies had three-foot (1-meter) wingspans.

Dragonflies are like acrobats. They whiz through the air at up to 60 mph (96 km/h). They can hover like helicopters. And, they eat while they are flying.

Roseate Skimmer Dragonfly.

Dragonflies have six legs and three body parts. They have large eyes that can see almost all the way around their bodies. Dragonflies come in many colors and sizes.

Male and female dragonflies.

The Dragonfly's Body

Dragonflies have three body sections: a head, a thorax, and an abdomen. The first section is the head. The middle section is the thorax. The last section is the abdomen.

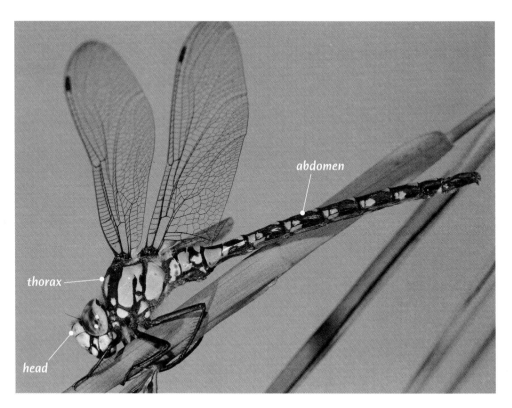

abdomen

thorax

head

On top of a dragonfly's head are two short antennae. The antennae sense movement. The antennae are not long because a dragonfly's sight is so keen. Dragonflies have huge, bulging compound eyes. Compound eyes have many lenses. People's eyes have only one lens to help them see. A dragonfly's eye has 30,000. Attached to the thorax are the dragonfly's wings.

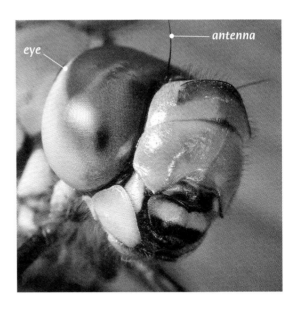

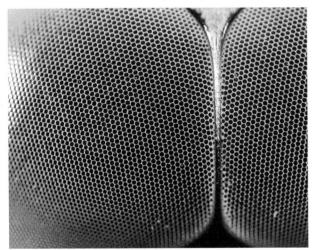

Close-up of a dragonfly's compound eyes.

Dragonflies have two sets of wings. They are clear and lined with veins. Unlike most insect wings, dragonfly wings can move independently. This allows the dragonfly to move quickly in the air. The dragonfly's three sets of legs are also on the thorax.

Dragonflies have a waterproof, translucent skin called an exoskeleton. Dragonflies have colorful skin. The beautiful blue, red, green, and yellow colors are in a layer of fat just under the skin. Metallic colors such as gold and bronze are on the skin's surface.

A dragonfly's heart pumps blood through a system of tubes called veins. You can see the veins in a dragonfly's wings. They look like thin black lines. Dragonflies need nutrients from blood to make their wings strong.

Dragonflies are cold-blooded. Their body temperature is always changing. If it is cold out, they are cold. If it is warm out, they are warm. If it gets too cold, dragonflies cannot fly. They have to wait until the sun warms them. Or, they beat their wings fast to warm up.

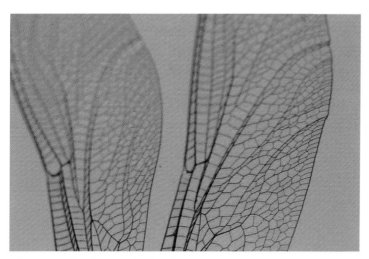

Close-up of a dragonfly's wings.

Inside the narrow abdomen is the gut. Here, mosquitoes, gnats, and other foods are ground up and digested. The abdomen also holds organs for mating.

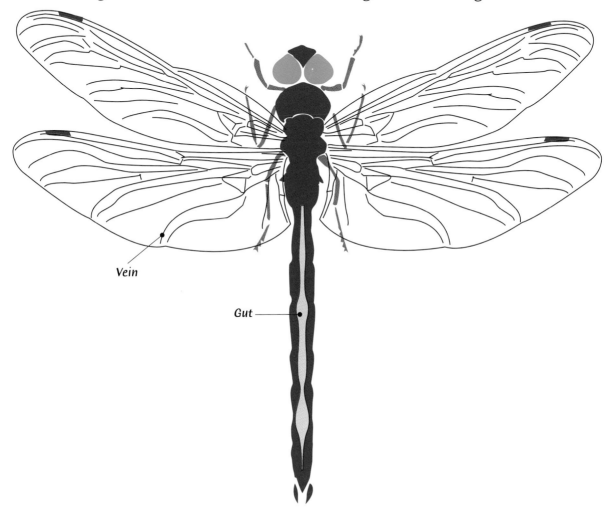

Vein

Gut

How They Grow

Dragonflies lay their eggs in or near water. They lay up to 100,000 at once. The eggs hatch in about a month. Baby dragonflies are called naiads. They live in the water. Naiads do not look like adult dragonflies. They do not have wings. They are not colorful.

Naiads are always hungry. They use their huge lower lip to catch prey. The lip is folded under the naiad's head. It has sharp pincers on the end. The lip is so large it covers almost all of the naiad's face. It is sometimes called a mask.

When a meal moves within the naiad's range, the naiad reaches out with its lip and grabs the prey in the pincers. The pincers hold the prey while the naiad eats it.

Dragonflies laying eggs.

10

Soon, a naiad eats so much, its skin is too tight. It sheds its old skin for a new, bigger skin. This is called molting. Naiads grow fast. They molt often.

Just before a naiad molts for the last time, it climbs out of the water on a stick or grass stem.

This naiad extends its pincers to catch food.

This dragonfly just molted for the last time.

This time when it molts, it is an adult. At first, its wings are wet. Soon, they dry and the dragonfly flies away.

What They Eat

Adult dragonflies are excellent hunters. Their powerful eyes can spot prey from 40 feet (12 m) away. Once a dragonfly spots its next meal, it folds its legs into a basket. The basket scoops prey into the dragonfly's mouth.

Dragonflies do not stop to scoop up their food. They catch and eat on the wing. This means that they eat while they are flying.

Dragonfly eating an insect.

Dragonflies mostly eat other insects. Mosquitoes, flies, gnats, and bees are common prey. Sometimes, dragonflies have bigger meals. Large dragonflies can swoop down and capture frogs and fish from ponds and lakes.

This dragonfly nymph is eating a small fish.

13

Where They Live

Dragonflies live all over the world. They live in Africa and Europe. They live in North America and South America. They also live in Asia. Dragonflies live in many different climates.

These dragonflies live in a meadow.

Some dragonflies live in deserts. Other dragonflies live in the mountains. But, most dragonflies live near water. Swamps, ponds, and other wetlands are home to swarms of gnats, mosquitoes, and other dragonfly prey.

Dragonflies live near water for other reasons, too. Dragonflies lay their eggs in or near water. And, naiads must live in water until they are ready to become adults.

This dragonfly lives near water.

Enemies

Dragonflies have many enemies. From egg to adult, dragonflies struggle to survive. The second a dragonfly egg hits water, it is in danger. Small wasps and other predators skim the water in search of dragonfly eggs.

This bird is eating a dragonfly.

Once an egg hatches into a naiad, it has new enemies. Fish, birds, water spiders, and newts love to eat naiads. Naiads protect themselves by swimming away. Some naiads protect themselves by blending into mud and leaves. This way, enemies cannot see them.

16

The most dangerous time for a dragonfly is when it molts for the last time. Birds, fish, and crocodiles eat the dragonflies while they wait for their wings to dry.

This dragonfly is caught in a spider's web.

Dragonflies & People

Some people are afraid of dragonflies. The word dragon makes them sound dangerous. But, dragonflies do not hurt people. They do not sting or bite. Dragonflies help people. Dragonflies eat mosquitoes, gnats, and other pests.

This dragonfly is eating an insect.

In many parts of the world, dragonflies are used as food. Some people eat them raw. Others cook them over a fire or fry them. Some people make naiads into soup.

In Asia, dragonflies are used in medicines. Some kinds of dragonflies are thought to cure sore throats and fever.

In some parts of the world, people use dragonflies in medicine and food.

Fun Facts

- Dragonflies can swivel their heads almost all the way around.

- Dragonflies are closely related to damselflies. Damselflies look like dragonflies, but have a skinnier abdomen and smaller eyes.

Damselfly.

Dragonflies spend most of their lives as naiads. A dragonfly is a naiad for up to five years. Once a naiad becomes an adult dragonfly, it lives less than a year.

The fastest dragonflies live in Australia. They can fly up to 35 mph (56 km/h).

The tiny elfin skimmer is the world's smallest dragonfly.

Dragonfly.

Glossary

antennae – sense organs attached to the top of an insect's head.

compound eyes – eyes that have many small lenses.

exoskeleton – the outer covering of an insect. All the muscles are attached to it and it protects the soft internal organs.

fossil – a part of a plant or animal from long ago that is found in the earth's crust.

molting – when an animal sheds its outer covering.

naiad – the nymph stage of a dragonfly; the stage between egg and adult.

predator – an animal that kills and eats other animals.

prey – animals that are eaten by predators.

translucent – something that light can pass through, but is not perfectly clear.

wingspan – the distance from one wing tip to the other when the wings spread.

Web Sites

Join the Bug Club
> http://www.ex.ac.uk/bugclub/
> This site for young entomologists includes a newsletter, puzzles, and games.

Worldwide Dragonfly Association
> http:powell.colgate.edu/wda/dragonfly.htm
> This site, hosted by Colgate University, includes extensive dragonfly information.

www.insecta.com/insecta/index.shtml

Index

To my forever family. I love you! —Sofia Sanchez

For my grandchildren. —Meg O'Hair

To my family. —Sofia Cardoso

Text copyright © 2023 by Margaret O'Hair

Illustrations copyright © 2023 by Scholastic Inc.

Photo credits: page 37 (top left): © Melissa Babasin Photography; page 37 (top right): © Jennifer Varanini Sanchez; page 37 (center): © Tiffany Green Photography & Designs; page 37 (bottom left): © Melissa Babasin Photography; page 37 (bottom right): © Jennifer Varanini Sanchez

Library of Congress Cataloging-in-Publication Data available

ISBN 978-1-338-85007-9

10 9 8 7 6 5 4 3 2 1   23 24 25 26 27

Printed in China   38

First edition, March 2023

Book design by Katie Fitch

Edited by Samantha Swank

you ARE loved

A BOOK ABOUT FAMILIES

Inspired by

SOFIA SANCHEZ

Written by Margaret O'Hair   Illustrated by Sofia Cardoso

Scholastic Inc.

My name is Sofia Sanchez. I live with my parents, my three older brothers, two dogs, and an orange kitty. Diego is my oldest brother. Mateo is the second oldest in my family. Joaquin is next. He is just one year older than me! They are my family.

My three brothers were born into my family. But I came into my family in a different way. My parents saw a picture of me when I was in an orphanage in Ukraine. I was just one year old.

My parents knew I was supposed to be in the Sanchez family. They traveled all the way across the globe to meet me. My mom and dad adopted me, and I chose them right back. That's how we became a family.

But my family is more than just the people I live with. I have family spread out all over the world!

My dad is named Hector. He was born in Mexico. I have many aunts, uncles, and cousins who still live there. We get to visit them a lot!

My mom's name is Jennifer. She was born in California. My grandparents live in the same town as us, and I have more aunts, uncles, and cousins nearby.

My family and I have lots of adventures together. We travel to new places, visit movie theaters and water parks, and go bowling and horseback riding. We hike and swim and walk our dogs.

Your family probably looks different from mine. That's okay, because all families are different. And there's not just one way to make a family. What matters is that you and your family love one another—just like mine does!

You are loved by so many people.

Your friends love you.

So do your neighbors and teachers.

Most of all you are loved by your family.

No one loves you like
your family loves you.

But what makes a family?

Family isn't just the people you are related to or the people you see every day.

Families are made with LOVE.

A family is something special. No two families look the same.

Sometimes you are born into your family.

Sometimes you choose your family.

And sometimes your family chooses you.

Family is the people who tell you things like:

Family is the people who are important to you—the people who love you just the way you are.

Families can be loud or quiet.

They can be big

or small

or somewhere
in between.

Sometimes the people in a family look the same.

Other families are made up of
lots of different kinds of people.

There's no right or wrong way to be a family.

What keeps a family together is **LOVE**.

Some families are lucky to live together under one roof.

Other families may be spread out across
a neighborhood, a country, or the world.

But family is about more than where you live.

Families are people who love and care for one another.

So even when you're away from your family,

you still carry them with you in your heart.

Some families spend lots of time together.

They celebrate together.

They eat and play and work together.

They know that they'll always be there to support one another, no matter what.

But families are not perfect.

Sometimes families **ARGUE**,

get **MAD**,
and get **SAD**.

Loving people can be hard.

But being a family means promising to make up and try again.

Families grow and change.

Babies are born

and kids grow up.

We meet new people who become part of our families.

And sometimes we lose people we love, too.

But no matter what your family looks like, one thing stays the same: how much you **LOVE** one another.

Parents, grandparents, and siblings.

Aunts, uncles, and cousins.

Friends, teachers, and neighbors.

Life is *so much better* when you have people to love—
and people who love you—by your side.

There's not just one way to make a family.

Families are born when you find the people
who make you HAPPY and help you feel STRONG.

The people who remind you,
"You belong. **YOU ARE LOVED.**"

A NOTE FROM SOFIA'S MOM

For as long as I can remember, all I ever wanted to be was a mom. I love children. I love family. I was so excited to create a family of my own.

I was blessed with three biological boys. It wasn't until giving birth to Joaquin, who has Down syndrome, that I realized there are children who don't have a family solely because they have a disability. That's when we opened our eyes to the possibility of adoption for our family.

Families are always changing, and ours changed when we found Sofia. When she came into our family, it was like she was always meant to be with us. We all fit together, and I can't imagine life any other way.

We are so lucky to have a community around us that has loved and supported us from the beginning. It truly takes a village, and when you do life right, your village can become family—the people you go to when life gets hard, and when you have moments to celebrate!

Thank you for being part of our family.

-Jennifer

FAMILY